BAD HAIR DAY

words&pictures

To my family—how blessed I am.
Thank you for your support and
encouragement over the years.
This is for you — J.P.

To my wonderful curly kids,
Margaux and Beau xxx — J.J.

Text © 2023 John Phillips
Illustrations © 2023 Jennifer Jamieson

John Phillips has asserted his right to be identified as the author of this work.
Jennifer Jamieson has asserted her right to be identified as the illustrator of this work.

First published in 2023 by words & pictures, an imprint of The Quarto Group.
100 Cummings Center, Suite 265D Beverly, MA 01915, USA.
T (978) 282-9590 F (978) 283-2742
www.quarto.com

A CIP record for this book is available from the Library of Congress.

ISBN: 978-0-7112-9016-7

Manufactured in in Guangdong, China TT072023
9 8 7 6 5 4 3 2 1

MIX
Paper | Supporting
responsible forestry
FSC® C016973
www.fsc.org

BAD HAIR DAY

words & pictures

Should have stayed tucked up in my bed...
Should have pulled the covers back over my head.

Instead I hit the floor,
headed for the door...
Just to hear my brother say...

MOUSSE AIN'T STICKIN',

WATER AIN'T SLICKIN',

IT LOOKS LIKE
A FEATHER

FROM THE BACK
END OF A CHICKEN.

I AIN'T GONNA USE NO <u>SILLY</u> HAIRSPRAY...

I'M HAVIN' SUCH A

BAD

HAIR

DAY!

Looked in the mirror, OH WHAT A SIGHT...
Must have been fighting with my pillow all night.

It got me in a tizz,
to see it in a frizz...

I couldn't find my gel
ANYWHERE.

I'M HAVIN' SUCH A

BAD

HAIR
DAY!

Opened up the cupboard,
feeling kinda stressed...

Try'na find **something**
that would fix this mess.

Suddenly my hair turned

GREEN!

Hopped off the bus with a plan in my head... Maybe I could hide it with a beanie instead.

Teacher saw the hat...

She said,
"YOU AIN'T WEARING THAT.
Remember what day it is today?"